FURNITURE 1800~1950

COMPILED BY TONY CURTIS

While every care has been taken in the compiling of information contained in this volume the publishers cannot accept any liability for loss, financial or otherwise, incurred by reliance placed on the information herein.

All prices quoted in this book are obtained from a variety of auctions in various countries and are converted to dollars at the rate of exchange prevalent at the time of sale.

ISBN 0-86248-007-8

INTRODUCTION

This book is one of a series specially devised to aid the busy professional dealer in his everyday trading. It will also prove to be of great value to all collectors and those with goods to sell, for it is crammed with illustrations, brief descriptions and valuations of hundreds of antiques.

Every effort has been made to ensure that each specialised volume contains the widest possible variety of goods in its particular category though the greatest emphasis is placed on the middle bracket of trade goods rather than on those once-in-a-lifetime museum pieces whose values are of academic rather than practical interest to the vast majority of dealers and collectors.

This policy has been followed as a direct consequence of requests from dealers who sensibly realise that, no matter how comprehensive their knowledge, there is always a need for reliable, up-to-date reference works for identification and valuation purposes.

When using your Antiques and their Values Book to assess the worth of goods, please bear in mind that it would be impossible to place upon any item a precise value which would hold good under all circumstances. No antique has an exactly calculable value; its price is always the result of a compromise reached between buyer and seller, and questions of condition, local demand and the business acumen of the parties involved in a sale are all factors which affect the assessment of an object's 'worth' in terms of hard cash.

In the final analysis, however, such factors cancel out when large numbers of sales are taken into account by an experienced valuer, and it is possible to arrive at a surprisingly accurate assessment of current values of antiques; an assessment which may be taken confidently to be a fair indication of the worth of an object and which provides a reliable basis for negotiation.

Throughout this book, objects are grouped under category headings and, to expedite reference, they progress in price order within their own categories. Where the description states 'one of a pair' the value given is that for the pair sold as such.

The publishers wish to express their sincere thanks
to the following for their kind help and assistance
in the production of this volume:

JANICE MONCRIEFF
NICOLA PARK
CARMEN MILIVOYEVICH
ELAINE HARLAND
MAY MUTCH
MARGOT RUTHERFORD
JENNIFER KNOX

Printed by Apollo Press, Worthing, Sussex, England.
Bound by R. J. Acford, Chichester, Sussex, England.

CONTENTS

Victorian mahogany single bed with panelled ends.
$280 £125

Regency mahogany folding campaign bed, 7ft. 4in. high. $450 £200

'Mouseman' oak bed by Robert Thompson, circa 1935, 39in. wide.
$495 £220

Brass half-tester bed, circa 1900, 76in. wide.
$565 £250

Victorian painted metal bed. $745 £330

Walnut half-tester bed, circa 1900, 83 x 58¼in.
$765 £340

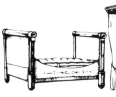

Empire mahogany single bed with panelled head and foot ends, 43¼in. wide. $1,170 £520

Late Victorian mahogany half-tester bed, complete with original drapes.
$1,170 £520

Early 19th century Dutch marquetry 'lit bateau', 3ft. 6in. wide. $1,295 £575

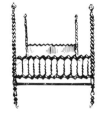

Mid 20th century softwood and simulated bamboo tester bed, 72¾in. long. $1,465 £650

Victorian mahogany bedstead. $1,530 £680

Old English tent bed in fruitwood with ogee shaped canopy, 3ft.3in. wide. $1,575 £700

Victorian mahogany double bunk bed with stairs to the upper tier. $1,630 £725

Giltwood and plaster bed, 19th century, 4ft. wide. $1,630 £725

Solid satinwood poster bed, foot posts reeded and garlanded, swags and decorations carved from solid posts, circa 1850, 5ft. wide, 8ft. high. $1,915 £850

19th century carved oak half-tester bed. $5,400 £2,400

19th century Venetian giltwood bed, 78in. wide. $5,400 £2,400

Mahogany and burl walnut double bed by Louis Majorelle, circa 1897, 68½in. wide. $12,375 £5,500

20th century oak book-
case, 20in. wide. $45 £20

Early 20th century oak
sectional bookcase.
$150 £65

Edwardian revolving book-
case of mahogany, 50cm.
wide. $450 £200

Simulated rosewood book-
case, circa 1840, 104in.
wide. $900 £400

Edwardian burr-maple
bookcase inlaid with ebony
and satinwood.
$1,070 £475

Red japanned chinoiserie
bookcase, doors applied
with gilt tooled book
spines, circa 1920.
$1,125 £500

Early 19th century
Regency mahogany revolv-
ing bookstand, 53in. high.
$3,600 £1,600

One of a pair of Regency
rosewood and brass inlaid
breakfront dwarf cabinets,
153cm. wide.
$4,165 £1,850

William IV pedestal book-
case in rosewood, 19½in.
high. $5,175 £2,300

19th century Victorian mahogany bookcase with glazed top, 230cm. high. $360 £160

Carved oak bookcase, 1860's, 31in. wide. $620 £275

William IV mahogany library bookcase with glazed top, 111cm. wide. $900 £400

19th century Continental oak bookcase. $1,465 £650

Late 19th century mahogany bookcase, 64in. wide. $1,685 £750

Carved oak bookcase, 1920's, 59in. wide, in the manner of Samuel Pepys' bookcases. $1,745 £775

Carved Victorian bookcase with open shelves. $2,250 £1,000

Mahogany bookcase of 'Strawberry Hill' design, 48in. wide. $2,250 £1,000

William IV carved mahogany library bookcase, 84in. wide. $2,250 £1,000

Victorian burr-walnut library bookcase, 49½in. wide. $2,475 £1,100

George III mahogany breakfront bookcase, 1890's, 95in. high. $2,700 £1,200

Mahogany bookcase with recessed centre cornice, circa 1830, 83¾in. wide. $2,925 £1,300

Dutch mahogany and marquetry bookcase, circa 1850, 33½in. wide. $3,040 £1,350

19th century carved oak breakfront bookcase. $3,375 £1,500

Victorian mahogany breakfront library bookcase, 6ft. 1in. wide. $3,510 £1,560

William IV carved mahogany library bookcase, 118in. wide.$3,600 £1,600

19th century Flemish carved oak bookcase cupboard, 4ft.10in. wide. $3,715 £1,650

Late Regency breakfront rosewood bookcase, 6ft. 6in. wide. $3,825 £1,700

Victorian mahogany break-
front bookcase.
$3,825 £1,700

George IV library book-
case, circa 1825, 6ft.2in.
wide. $3,940 £1,750

19th century mahogany
bookcase, 5ft.8in. wide.
$4,840 £2,150

Edwardian mahogany and
satinwood marquetry in-
laid breakfront library
bookcase, 6ft.3in. wide.
$5,625 £2,500

Early 19th century maho-
gany arch top library breakfront bookcase, 99in. high.
$6,950 £3,000

Victorian walnut bookcase
with shaped glazed doors.
$6,975 £3,100

Breakfront mahogany book-
case with marquetry motifs
on cornice, 9ft. high.
$6,975 £3,100

Early 19th century library
bookcase. $19,690 £8,750

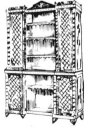

Regency mahogany book-
case by G. Oakley, 78½in.
wide. $20,250 £9,000

20th century oak bureau with oxidised handles. $170 £75

An Edwardian mahogany inlaid bureau with folding over writing board and three long drawers, 2ft.6in. wide. $450 £200

19th century Burmese hardwood bureau with arched and incised legs, 71cm. wide.$495 £220

19th century stripped pine bureau on bracket feet, with brass handles, 3ft. wide. $505 £225

Louis XV style kingwood bureau de dame with brass gallery, 67cm. wide. $855 £380

Carved oak bureau, circa 1880, 45¼in. wide. $1,015 £450

Edwardian mahogany bureau with crossbanded fall flap, 23in. wide. $1,080 £480

Burr-walnut corner bureau on cabriole legs, circa 1920. $1,080 £480

Georgian mahogany bureau of good colour, 3ft. wide. $1,295 £575

19th century Oriental carved teak bureau.
$1,350 £600

Mahogany bureau de dame with pierced gallery and marble top, circa 1900, 32¼in. wide.
$1,395 £620

Late 19th century rosewood and floral marquetry bureau de dame, 26in. wide.
$1,530 £680

Vernis Martin bureau a cylindre, circa 1900, 31½in. wide, with brown marble top. $1,690 £750

Early 19th century German mahogany cylinder bureau, 3ft.6in. wide. $1,800 £800

19th century Dutch colonial block-fronted bureau, 92cm. wide. $1,970 £875

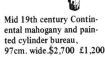

Late 19th century king-wood and tulipwood bureau a cylindre with marble top, 34½in. wide.
$2,365 £1,050

Mid 19th century Continental mahogany and painted cylinder bureau, 97cm. wide. $2,700 £1,200

19th century Dutch marquetry and walnut bombe-shaped lady's bureau, 90cm. wide.
$3,375 £1,500

15

Late 19th century American desk by Wootton Desk Co., Indianapolis.
$3,600 £1,600

Satinwood and marquetry cylinder bureau, late 19th century, 47½in. wide.
$4,950 £2,200

19th century floral marquetry cylinder bureau with revolving top, 113cm. wide.
$4,950 £2,200

19th century Dutch marquetry bureau, 33in. wide.
$5,625 £2,500

American 'Wells Fargo' desk by Wootton & Co., 42½in. wide.
$6,750 £3,000

Viennese ormolu mounted mahogany cylinder bureau, circa 1825, 2ft.6in. wide.
$7,200 £3,200

Late 19th century satinwood and marquetry cylinder bureau, 36in. wide.
$9,000 £4,000

19th century writing desk with Swiss orchestral musical movement.
$9,450 £4,200

French marquetry bureau a cylindre, 19th century, 32½in. wide.
$20,085 £9,250

20th century oak bureau
bookcase with H stretcher.
$335 £150

Edwardian mahogany bur-
eau bookcase with glazed
doors enclosing adjustable
shelves. $450 £200

Victorian cylinder secre-
taire bookcase in mahogany.
$675 £300

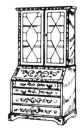

Late 19th century maho-
gany bureau bookcase, 36in.
wide. $675 £300

Mid 19th century Contin-
ental mahogany cylinder
bureau with bookshelves
above. $675 £300

Late 19th century oak bureau bookcase, 78in. high.
$900 £400

19th century oak bureau
bookcase on bracket feet.
$1,350 £600

Mahogany bureau book-
case, circa 1920, 3ft.6in.
wide. $1,350 £600

Early 19th century maho-
gany bureau bookcase with
astragal glazed doors.
$1,915 £850

BUREAU BOOKCASES

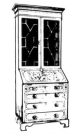

Late 19th century satinwood bureau cabinet, 24½in. wide. $1,620 £720

Victorian bureau bookcase with glazed upper half. $1,970 £875

Edwardian bureau bookcase with astragal doors and satinwood inlay, 33in. wide. $2,025 £900

'Renaissance' walnut and parquetry bureau cabinet stamped Edwards & Roberts, 1880's, 42in. wide. $2,475 £1,100

Sneezewood estate bureau bookcase, early 20th century, made in South Africa. $2,590 £1,150

19th century walnut veneered Queen Anne style double domed bureau bookcase. $2,590 £1,150

Edwardian bureau bookcase in mahogany with satinwood banding. $2,700 £1,200

Regency rosewood writing cabinet with a raised and painted mirror back. $2,815 £1,250

19th century floral marquetry bureau bookcase on cabriole legs. $2,815 £1,250

18

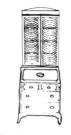

Late 19th century mahogany bureau bookcase, 30in. wide. $3,150 £1,400

19th century satinwood bureau bookcase of Sheraton design, 2ft.11in. wide. $3,150 £1,400

Early 19th century Chinese export lacquer bureau cabinet, 33in. wide. $3,265 £1,450

Regency kingwood bureau cabinet, inlaid on the front and sides. $3,375 £1,500

Edwardian walnut secretaire bureau bookcase. $3,825 £1,700

Regency mahogany cylinder bureau bookcase, circa 1810, 3ft.8in. wide. $5,175 £2,300

Early 19th century Dutch marquetry bureau cabinet, 42in. wide. $6,750 £3,000

19th century marquetry bureau cabinet. $10,125 £4,500

Early 19th century Dutch marquetry bureau cabinet, with a bombe front. $13,500 £6,000

19

CABINETS

Art Nouveau style beech-wood music cabinet.
$100 £45

Late 19th century walnut side cabinet. $190 £85

Edwardian inlaid mahogany music cabinet with fall-front drawers. $225 £100

Late 19th century bamboo music cabinet. $305 £135

Victorian inlaid walnut wood cabinet surmounted with oval mirror, 24in. wide. $350 £155

Ebonised cabinet in the style of Gillow & Co., 104cm. wide, circa 1880. $360 £160

English mahogany and painted 'Gothic' side cabinet, 1890's, 38in. wide. $610 £270

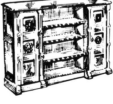

Solid walnut side cabinet, mid 1870's, 73in. wide. $620 £275

Liberty & Co. tall oak side cabinet, circa 1920, 26in. wide. $620 £275

Ebonised beechwood brass inlaid meuble d'appui, circa 1870, 42¾in. wide.
$630 £280

19th century mahogany apothecary's cabinet.
$655 £290

German walnut side cabinet in well figured wood, 38½in. wide, 1950's. $675 £300

19th century carved oak cabinet in 'Gothic' style, 82cm. wide. $730 £325

Small Art Nouveau breakfront cabinet, circa 1900, 58in. wide. $730 £325

Edwardian satin walnut cabinet with painted decoration. $745 £330

Victorian burr-walnut music cabinet, on turned legs, 41in. high. $810 £360

Oriental lacquer cabinet on stand. $900 £400

Mahogany Art Nouveau side cabinet, inlaid throughout with foliage, 83in. high.
$900 £400

CABINETS

Mahogany collector's cabinet, 1860's, 49¾in. high.
$925 £410

Walnut dental cabinet, circa 1890, figured in burrwood, 29¼in. wide.
$990 £440

19th century Japanese lacquer cabinet, 19in. high.
$1,195 £530

Satinwood bow-fronted side cabinet, 3ft.4in. wide.
$1,195 £530

Satinwood side cabinet with swan neck cresting, circa 1890, 86in. high.
$1,240 £550

19th century walnut and tulipwood side cabinet, 33in. wide. $1,240 £550

An Art Nouveau mahogany cabinet in the Liberty style, 110cm. wide.
$1,305 £580

Stylish 1930's cocktail cabinet in pale walnut, 144cm. wide.
$1,485 £660

19th century ornate carved walnut cabinet, 82cm. wide.
$1,745 £775

Early 19th century Dutch
colonial satinwood, ebony
and coromandelwood
cabinet, 4ft.7in. wide.
$1,800 £800

Breakfront ebonised, gilt
bronze and pietra dura side
cabinet, with black slate
top, circa 1850, 78in.
wide. $2,140 £950

Japanese black lacquer display cabinet on stand,
77cm. wide. $2,140 £950

Carved oak side cabinet,
with lower part made from
a commode, circa 1850-80,
42in. wide. $3,265 £1,450

19th century French ebony
and marquetry cabinet,
45¼in. wide. $5,515 £2,450

19th century Japanese Shibayama cabinet.
$8,100 £3,600

Rare Godwin ebonised
mahogany aesthetic cabinet,
circa 1869, 96in. high.
$14,625 £6,500

Fine Meissen and ebony
cabinet, Dresden 1870.
$45,000 £20,000

Writing cabinet of dark
stained wood by Charles
Rennie Mackintosh, 37¼in.
wide. $180,000 £80,000

Victorian bamboo canterbury with lacquered panels. $55 £25

A Victorian mahogany canterbury with fretted partitions. $420 £185

Victorian burr-walnut canterbury with shaped oval inlaid table top. $765 £340

Regency rosewood canterbury with drawer, 48cm. wide. $900 £400

Victorian burr-walnut canterbury. $900 £400

19th century rosewood four division canterbury, 49cm. wide.$900 £400

George III mahogany canterbury on slender turned tapered legs.$1,800 £800

Early 19th century mahogany canterbury 'whatnot' with bookrest top. $2,250 £1,000

Regency mahogany canterbury with eight divisions, 43in. wide.$3,265 £1,450

One of a set of six 20th century oak dining chairs. $125 £50

One of a pair of ebonised side chairs, 1870's. $145 £65

One of a pair of Art Deco giltwood chairs, 94cm. high. $190 £85

One of a set of four Edwardian carved mahogany chairs. $270 £120

One of a set of six Austrian oak dining chairs, circa 1900. $315 £140

One of a set of four Edwardian inlaid mahogany chairs. $315 £140

One of a pair of oak dining chairs by Alfred Waterhouse, 1870's, $340 £150

One of a set of four English mahogany side chairs with carved heads and armorial cartouches, 1870's. $430 £190

One of six late 19th century ebonised beechwood dining chairs. $450 £200

DINING CHAIRS

One of a set of four walnut chairs, circa 1830.
$450 £200

One of a pair of ebonised and ivory side chairs, circa 1880. $450 £200

One of a set of six 19th century mahogany dining chairs with shaped top rails. $495 £220

One of a set of six Austrian bentwood dining chairs, stamped Thonet, circa 1920. $495 £220

One of a set of six late 19th century mahogany framed dining chairs. $505 £225

One of a pair of Bettridge & Co. black papier mache boudoir chairs.
$565 £250

One of a pair of 19th century rosewood and marquetry chairs. $645 £285

One of a pair of Regency hall chairs with shell backs. $655 £290

One of a set of four 19th century rosewood dining chairs with scrolled balloon backs. $720 £320

One of a set of six mahogany dining chairs, circa 1840. $745 £330

One of a set of six Flemish carved oak dining chairs, circa 1880. $765 £340

One of a set of six Biedermeier fruitwood chairs, circa 1830. $865 £385

One of a set of six early 20th century walnut dining chairs. $900 £400

One of a pair of late 19th century Dutch mahogany and marquetry side chairs. $1,035 £460

One of a set of ten mahogany dining chairs, 18th/ 19th century, possibly Anglo-Chinese. $1,125 £500

One of a set of six walnut drawingroom chairs, 1860's. $1,125 £500

One of a set of six Regency ebonised dining chairs, Scottish. $1,170 £520

One of a set of six German mahogany veneered dining chairs, 1840's. $1,240 £550

DINING CHAIRS

One of a set of four satinwood dining chairs painted with flowers, circa 1900.
$1,305 £580

One of a set of six English rosewood drawingroom chairs, circa 1860.
$1,305 £580

19th century richly carved baroque chair in oak, covered with silk.
$1,365 £610

One of a set of six early 19th century French provincial cherrywood dining chairs with rush seats.
$1,365 £610

One of a set of ten oak dining chairs, circa 1850.
$1,485 £660

One of a set of six 19th century French dining chairs with padded backs.
$1,545 £685

One of a set of nine handsome Victorian carved oak dining chairs with cane seats. $1,575 £700

One of a set of six painted and giltwood chairs, late 19th century, partly upholstered in petit point.
$1,575 £700

One of a set of seven Regency beechwood chairs, with an X-shaped splat.
$1,690 £750

One of a set of four Dutch marquetry dining chairs, circa 1810. $1,690 £750

One of a set of eight Victorian rosewood single chairs. $1,800 £800

One of a set of six simulated rosewood Regency dining chairs.
$2,700 £1,200

Bugatti swingback chair, circa 1900, 101cm. high, sides covered in vellum.
$3,825 £1,700

One of a pair of silver gilt and silver veneered throne chairs, circa 1880.
$4,615 £2,050

One of a set of eight Regency ebonised and gilded dining chairs. $6,750 £3,000

Straight backed chair designed by Frank Lloyd, circa 1910-16, 81.5cm. high. $6,750 £3,000

Oak high back chair designed by Charles Rennie Mackintosh, 1897.
$10,800 £4,800

One of a set of twelve mahogany dining chairs, 19th century. $12,375 £5,500

Late Victorian oak easy chair with padded arms. $55 £25

Edwardian wickerwork easy chair with ribbed seat and back. $55 £25

Victorian deep buttoned tub chair on turned oak legs. $100 £45

A Victorian mahogany tub chair on cabriole legs. $100 £45

Victorian rosewood bergere chair on brass castors. $170 £75

Victorian Abbotsford chair with needlework upholstery. $225 £100

A Victorian carved walnut high back armchair on turned legs. $280 £125

Dentist's chair upholstered in leather, circa 1910-15. $280 £125

19th century rosewood framed armchair with carved cresting rail. $450 £200

Large Art Deco giltwood
tub chair, early 1920's.
$495 £220

Walnut armchair, circa
1920, with seat and back in
needlepoint. $540 £240

19th century highly carved
hardwood easy chair.
$540 £240

Military officer's conver-
tible chair-bed in iron
and brass, circa 1840-60.
$565 £250

Victorian steel-framed
rocking chair with
leather upholstery.
$565 £250

Unusual painted beech-
wood throne armchair,
Italian, circa 1880.
$620 £275

Mid Victorian upholstered
walnut lady's chair with
cabriole legs, 35in. high.
$665 £295

Italian walnut crinoline
chair, circa 1830.
$675 £300

Fritz Hansens 'egg' chair,
105.5cm. high, on alumi-
nium base. $675 £300

31

EASY CHAIRS

English walnut armchair with crested back and serpentine seat on cabriole legs, circa 1860. $745 £330

One of a pair of Art Deco tub chairs, early 1920's. $765 £340

English walnut button-back armchair with moulded frame and serpentine seat, circa 1860. $880 £390

One of a pair of Anglo-Indian ebony armchairs, mid 19th century. $900 £400

One of a pair of Italian or South German walnut side chairs, circa 1850. $900 £400

Charles X inlaid pollard-elm bergere, circa 1820. $990 £440

Asko fibreglass 'globe' chair, 125cm. diam. $990 £440

Victorian oak rocking chair. $1,125 £500

Herman Miller lounge chair, 82cm. high, designed by Charles Eames. $1,350 £600

Early 19th century rose-
wood armchair, uphol-
stered in leather.
$1,690 £750

Victorian laminated rose-
wood armchair with carved
crest and pierced back.
$2,025 £900

One of a pair of Regency
mahogany bergeres with
padded backs and leather
seats, on X frames.
$2,140 £950

One of a pair of Swedish
giltwood bergeres with husk-
carved arms, circa 1800.
$3,150 £1,400

French 19th century sedan
chair lacquered cabinet
embellished with ormolu
mounts in the style of
Vernis Martin, 51½in. high,
22½in. wide, 18½in. deep.
$3,375 £1,500

One of a pair of 20th century 'Louis XVI' giltwood
fauteuils. $3,490 £1,550

One of a pair of Regency
mahogany bergeres with
caned backs, sides and
seats. $5,625 £2,500

One of a pair of armchairs
by Jacques Rhulmann,
circa 1925 $8,440 £3,750

American library armchair
attributed to Duncan
Phyfe, circa 1815.
$33,750 £15,000

33

ELBOW CHAIRS

Early 20th century oak rush-seated elbow chair.
$45 £20

A child's chair, Russian, 1850's, 26½in. high.
$90 £40

Victorian beechwood smoker's chair with saddle seat.　$100 £45

A Colonial carved oak armchair, by Edwards & Roberts.　$115 £50

Late 19th century mahogany swivel chair with pierced splat. $160 £70

19th century carved mahogany corner chair.
$160 £70

Liberty & Co. oak armchair, circa 1900.
$170 £75

20th century Carine parquetry armchair.
$170 £75

Late 19th century inlaid mahogany elbow chair.
$170 £75

Oak and elm 19th century spindleback chair with curved arms. $180 £80

Late 19th century child's turned beechwood rocking chair. $215 £95

Mid 19th century English oak X-framed leather upholstered armchair. $215 £95

Early 19th century Chippendale style mahogany elbow chair on ball and claw feet. $340 £150

Italian style rocking chair with ladder back and leather embossed seat. $340 £150

Early 20th century walnut Burgomaster chair. $370 £165

Highly carved 19th century Oriental hardwood elbow chair. $395 £175

An Italian walnut and ivory Savonarola armchair, circa 1860. $395 £175

An early 20th century Dutch walnut marquetry armchair. $450 £200

ELBOW CHAIRS

19th century Continental carved walnut X-framed elbow chair in Renaissance style. $475 £210

Mid 19th century walnut 'grotto' armchair. $520 £230

Early 20th century Dutch marquetry corner chair. $555 £245

Scottish mahogany armchair, circa 1900. $575 £255

Anglo-Indian ebony armchair, circa 1830, with caned back and seat. $585 £260

Mid 18th century Windsor armchair in elm and yewwood, on turned legs with crinoline stretcher. $585 £260

George IV caned mahogany library chair, circa 1820. $720 £320

Late 19th century Scottish mahogany armchair painted by Rosie Morison, 61 in. high. $790 £350

Empire mahogany fauteuil with stuffed back, circa 1815. $865 £385

36

Bugatti throne armchair in ebonised wood, circa 1895, 140cm. high. $1,080 £480

Empire mahogany armchair, circa 1810. $1,015 £450

Regency carved oak rail-back armchair. $1,125 £500

19th century Korean cinnabar lacquer and gilded open armchair with leather seat. $1,350 £600

Mahogany elbow chair, probably Continental and early 19th century, with floral marquetry inlay. $1,350 £600

Buffalo horn armchair by W. Friedrich, Texas. $1,575 £700

Small oak rush-seated armchair by George Walton, circa 1900. $2,025 £900

German Regency beech-wood open armchair with caned back. $2,250 £1,000

Silver and silver veneered throne chair, 45in. wide, circa 1880. $10,350 £4,600

CHESTS OF DRAWERS

An Edwardian walnut chest of drawers with pierced brass handles. $90 £40

Pine watchmaker's chest with brass handles, 17in. high, circa 1880. $100 £45

Late 19th century walnut chest on a plinth base. $170 £75

Early 19th century mahogany chest on splay feet. $225 £100

20th century Jacobean style oak chest of drawers. $250 £110

A Victorian mahogany bow-front chest of three long and two short graduated cock beaded drawers, 3ft. 6in. wide. $280 £125

A 19th century mahogany and walnut chest of four long drawers, on bracket feet, 2ft.4in. wide. $340 £150

Late 19th century mahogany specimen chest on tapered legs with spade feet. $340 £150

Early 19th century mahogany bow-front chest of three long drawers. $505 £225

Victorian mahogany campaign chest of two halves with inset brass handles, 40in. wide. $520 £230

Mid 19th century painted chest of seven drawers, with a marble top. $540 £240

Art Deco burl maple chest of drawers, circa 1925, 51¾in. wide. $265 £250

Small mahogany chest of drawers, 2ft.9in. wide, circa 1810. $640 £285

Mahogany Wellington chest of drawers, 1870's, 22¾in. wide. $640 £285

Quaint poker work chest of drawers, signed by Laura Allsop, 35in. wide x 32in. high, circa 1845. $675 £300

Chest of drawers designed by Gordon Russell, circa 1930, 45in. high. $700 £310

Biedermeier satinwood chest of drawers, circa 1825, 3ft. wide. $900 £400

19th century Italian carved walnut chest, 5ft. wide. $1,000 £440

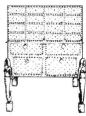

French mahogany chest of drawers of unusual design, ormolu mounts, 36in. wide, 33in. high, circa 1850.
$1,015 £450

French Provincial walnut veneered chest of drawers, Charles X period, circa 1820. $1,015 £450

19th century Eastern inlaid teak chest supported by four mermaids.
$1,105 £490

French mahogany chest of drawers with original ormolu mounts and handles, 38in. wide, circa 1850. $1,240 £550

Art Deco burl maple chest of drawers, 63¾in. high.
$1,260 £560

19th century walnut military chest of drawers, 99cm. wide.
$1,350 £600

Small antique walnut Wellington chest of seven drawers, 23in. wide.
$1,395 £620

Arts and Crafts Movement amboyna and satinwood chest of drawers, 2ft.9in. high x 2ft.7½in. wide x 1ft.10in. deep.
$1,405 £625

Early 19th century French rosewood bow-fronted chest of drawers with marble top, 24in. wide.
$1,690 £750

Regency period camphorwood secretaire military chest. $1,690 £750

Late 19th century floral marquetry inlaid mahogany chest.
      $1,745 £775

Dutch provincial bombe fronted chest on paw feet, circa 1840. $2,025 £900

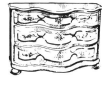

Early 19th century Dutch walnut and marquetry chest of drawers, 36in. wide. $2,475 £1,100

18th century South German walnut chest.
    $3,490 £1,550

Early 19th century Dutch marquetry bombe shaped chest of drawers, 37in. wide. $3,490 £1,550

Camphorwood chest of nine drawers and secretaire plus galleried decoration. $3,600 £1,600

Early 19th century French mahogany semainier with white marble top, 37in. wide. $3,600 £1,600

Serpentine fronted Dutch chest of drawers, circa 1800, 38in. high.
     $4,500 £2,000

41

CHEST ON CHEST

A Victorian maplewood and simulated bamboo chest of six drawers, 35in. wide. $900 £400

George III mahogany tallboy with original handles, 47½in. wide. $1,240 £550

Mid 19th century Georgian design mahogany bow-fronted tallboy, 112cm. wide. $1,300 £580

Late George III mahogany tallboy, circa 1805, 3ft. 10in. wide. $1,465 £650

George III mahogany tallboy with fluted decoration, circa 1800, 110cm. wide. $1,575 £700

Early 19th century walnut chest on chest, of small proportions, 36in. wide. $1,915 £850

19th century figured mahogany tallboy, 42in. high. $2,025 £900

Early 19th century mahogany tallboy, 3ft. wide. $2,700 £1,200

19th century oak and walnut cabinet on chest, heavily carved, 50in. wide. $2,700 £1,200

42

19th century inlaid mahogany chest on tapered legs. $225 £100

Edwardian Sheraton style narrow chest of drawers. $630 £280

Early 19th century walnut chest on stand. $630 £280

Chinoiserie cabinet on stand, circa 1920, 39½in. wide. $955 £425

George III oak chest on stand. $1,015 £450

19th century carved oak cabinet on stand, in the French Gothic style. $1,015 £450

Early 19th century simulated walnut chest on stand, 2ft.8in. wide. $1,465 £650

19th century marquetry chest in William and Mary style. $2,835 £1,260

Late 19th century German Dresden mounted side cabinet on stand. $24,750 £11,000

Late 19th century oak chiffonier. $65 £30

Late Victorian mahogany chiffonier with arched panel doors. $190 £85

Late 19th century mahogany chiffonier. $335 £150

Victorian rosewood chiffonier, 45in. wide. $505 £225

Small Georgian mahogany chiffonier, 40in. wide, circa 1830. $565 £250

Early 19th century figured mahogany chiffonier with panelled doors. $620 £275

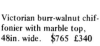

Victorian burr-walnut chiffonier with marble top, 48in. wide. $765 £340

Early 19th century rosewood chiffonier with unusual fretted door panels, 15½in. deep, 54in. wide, 49in. tall. $900 £400

Mid 19th century rosewood chiffonier with two-tier back, 45in. wide. $900 £400

Large Edwardian rosewood chiffonier, 8ft.6in. high. $1,080 £480

Regency chiffonier in rosewood, circa 1820, 36in. wide. $1,180 £525

Regency mahogany chiffonier with scroll supports. $1,350 £600

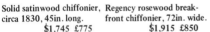

Solid satinwood chiffonier, circa 1830, 45in. long. $1,745 £775

Regency rosewood breakfront chiffonier, 72in. wide. $1,915 £850

William IV rosewood chiffonier. $2,025 £900

Regency brass inlaid rosewood chiffonier, 2ft.9in. wide, circa 1810. $3,490 £1,550

Late George III mahogany chiffonier, circa 1800, 2ft. 3in. wide, with graduated top. $4,950 £2,200

Regency rosewood chiffonier with concave outline. $4,950 £2,200

COMMODE CHESTS

19th century boxwood strung floral marquetry inlaid kingwood commode, 2ft.2in. wide. $810 £360

Biedermeier fruitwood commode with panelled ebonised frieze, circa 1820, 4ft. wide. $945 £420

Early 19th century French provincial kingwood petite commode, 41cm. high. $1,125 £500

Spanish mahogany commode with white marble top, circa 1825, 4ft.1in. wide. $1,685 £750

19th century Adam style demi-lune commode inlaid and painted with scrolling motifs, by Edwards & Roberts. $1,845 £820

French provincial walnut commode, circa 1810. $1,980 £880

Empire mahogany commode with black marble top, 51½in. wide. $2,475 £1,100

Late Georgian mahogany commode with two drawers. $2,725 £1,210

An ornate French 19th century commode with ebonised ormolu mounting. $2,815 £1,250

46

'Louis XV' style kingwood floral marquetry commode with marble top, 126cm. wide. $2,925 £1,300

Edwards & Roberts mid 19th century marble top Louis XVI style commode in rosewood, 80cm. wide. $3,150 £1,400

One of a pair of Biedermeier bird's eye maple commodes, 41in. wide. $3,715 £1,650

Edwardian satinwood commode with convex centre section. $4,275 £1,900

19th century French kingwood commode. $4,725 £2,100

19th century marquetry commode with floral decoration. $6,185 £2,750

Mid 19th century ebonised and marquetry commode. $10,125 £4,500

One of a pair of harewood and marquetry commodes with moulded marble tops, circa 1900, 46in. wide. $17,550 £7,800

Regency boulle commode en tombeau. $30,375 £13,500

47

Victorian bamboo and cane pot cupboard. $65 £30

Victorian mahogany commode complete with liner. $80 £35

Edwardian inlaid mahogany bedside cupboard. $80 £35

19th century French walnut pot cupboard on shaped legs. $135 £60

19th century mahogany lift-up commode with shaped apron. $170 £75

Victorian mahogany pot cupboard with fluted sides. $225 £100

Mahogany bedside table, circa 1800, 31in. high, with slatted shelf. $370 £165

Unconverted night commode, circa 1800, 28in. high. $385 £170

One of a pair of Regency mahogany bedside cupboards, circa 1805, 1ft.4in. wide. $1,575 £700

19th century mahogany corner cupboard enclosing three shaped shelves.
$80 £35

Ebonised mahogany corner cupboard, circa 1880, 115cm. high. $170 £75

A carved oak corner cupboard, the panel door with inlaid motifs of shell and print. $280 £125

Late 19th century satin walnut corner cabinet.
$295 £130

Inlaid bow-fronted corner display cupboard.
$295 £130

Victorian carved oak corner cupboard with broken arch pediment. $450 £200

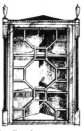

Edwardian inlaid mahogany corner cupboard on tapered legs with spade feet.
$450 £200

Small mahogany corner cupboard with brass gallery, 1890's, 33½ x 20in.
$600 £265

Walnut open corner cupboard, circa 1860, 72 x 29in. $765 £340

49

19th century French king-
wood and walnut veneered
encoignure, 28½in. wide.
$900 £400

19th century Dutch floral
marquetry corner cup-
board. $965 £430

Early 19th century oak
and mahogany double cor-
ner cupboard.
        $1,015 £450

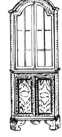

Late 19th century satin-
wood standing corner dis-
play cabinet, 42in. wide.
        $1,125 £500

Satinwood corner cabinet,
circa 1900, with inlaid
top and door.
        $1,195 £530

Walnut veneered early 19th
century glazed corner cupboard. $1,195 £530

Inlaid corner display cabinet. $1,400 £625

Early 19th century Georgian
design standing mahogany
corner cupboard, 120cm.
wide. $1,620 £720

Mahogany Regency corner
cupboard, 36in. wide,
circa 1820. $1,685 £750

19th century Breton style cradle, with turned finials, 90cm. wide. $160 £70

Victorian cast iron cradle on castors. $180 £80

19th century mahogany crib with carved end, 97cm. long. $245 £110

A 19th century Indian cradle. $340 £150

A Victorian brass crib.
          $340 £150

Regency caned mahogany cradle, 3ft.11in. high, circa 1820. $730 £325

George IV mahogany cradle, 3ft.1in. wide, circa 1825.
          $945 £420

Early 19th century parcel gilt mahogany cradle, 3ft. 11in. wide. $1,080 £480

Mid 19th century painted cradle, 38½in. long.
          $1,240 £550

51

Ebonised and burr-walnut side cabinet, 58in. wide, circa 1860. $520 £230

Mid 19th century walnut side cabinet, 67in. wide. $720 £320

Victorian rosewood credenza with carved framed mirror back, white marble top and centre glazed door, cupboard flanked by six mirror backed open shelves. $785 £350

19th century rosewood breakfront credenza with shaped back and barley twist columns. $1,465 £650

Victorian burr-walnut breakfront credenza with canted corners, 5ft.7in. wide. $1,690 £750

Walnut side cabinet, circa 1870, 4ft.9in. wide. $1,780 £790

Ebonised porcelain and gilt bronze mounted display cabinet, 1860's, 72in. wide. $1,980 £880

Victorian walnut credenza with concave ends and a glazed centre door. $2,700 £1,200

Burr-walnut side cabinet, 1860's, 72in. wide. $3,600 £1,600

Mid 19th century walnut credenza with marquetry designs. $3,940 £1,750

19th century boulle and ormolu credenza, 7ft. wide. $4,500 £2,000

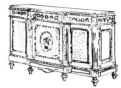

Marquetry meuble d'appui with breakfront white marble top, 1860's, 78in. wide. $4,615 £2,050

19th century Flanders carved oak neo-Gothic credenza. $4,695 £2,085

Walnut side cabinet, 1880's, 76in. wide. $4,950 £2,200

Marquetry kingwood porcelain mounted side cabinet, circa 1870, 82in. wide. $5,625 £2,500

Mid Victorian walnut and marquetry side cabinet by Gillows. $13,500 £6,000

53

19th century French fruit-wood bedside cupboard. $135 £60

Late 19th century oak side table with cupboard. $180 £80

Late Victorian carved oak buffet. $450 £200

Mahogany and oak linen press, 50in. wide. $600 £270

Biedermeier fruitwood cupboard, circa 1830, 3ft.8in. wide. $675 £300

20th century Jacobean style oak court cupboard. $730 £325

19th century Flemish tridarn cupboard, 34in. wide. $845 £375

Stained oak 'Gothick' low cupboard, 1860's, 39in. wide. $900 £400

Bleached oak court cupboard, 57in. wide, circa 1860. $1,015 £450

19th century Colonial carved teak linen press, 48in. wide. $1,185 £525

Regency walnut cupboard with moulded top, circa 1730, 4ft.7in. wide. $1,755 £780

Mid 19th century carved oak cupboard, 145cm. wide. $1,755 £780

19th century French carved oak cupboard on a stand, 48in. wide. $2,025 £900

19th century Flanders carved neo-renaissance cupboard in oak. $3,265 £1,450

Flemish oak bookcase cupboard, 19th century. $3,715 £1,650

Early 19th century French provincial cherrywood cupboard with shaped panel doors. $4,165 £1,850

Art Nouveau mahogany sideboard cupboard, French, circa 1900, 59in. wide. $7,650 £3,400

French Napoleon III period cupboard inlaid with pewter, brass and red tortoiseshell. $19,800 £8,800

DAVENPORTS

Oak Davenport with three-quarter gallery, 1880's, 24in. wide. $600 £265

Walnut Davenport writing table, circa 1870, 20¾in. wide. $675 £300

Mid 19th century walnut Davenport, 32 x 23½in. $675 £300

Walnut Davenport, circa 1860, 37½in. wide, with central turned balustrade. $745 £330

Regency Davenport of mahogany surmounted by a letter tray, 76cm. wide. $765 £340

Marquetry and rosewood Davenport with hinged superstructure, 21in. wide, circa 1900. $790 £350

Rosewood Davenport, 1870's, with leather-lined top, 20¾in. wide. $970 £430

Mahogany Davenport with pierced brass gallery, 33½in. wide, circa 1830. $1,015 £450

Victorian rosewood Davenport, with serpentine front, 53cm. wide. $1,095 £485

Late Victorian rosewood and marquetry Davenport. $1,465 £650

Victorian rosewood piano top Davenport, 25in. wide. $1,575 £700

Regency rosewood Davenport surmounted by a brass gallery, 17in. wide. $1,575 £700

Boulle Davenport with brass and gilt metal decoration, 21in. wide. $1,690 £750

Olivewood Davenport, top stencilled Jerusalem, circa 1880-1900, 29in. wide. $1,690 £750

Mid Victorian walnut Davenport with gallery top. $2,025 £900

William IV rosewood Davenport, circa 1830, 1ft.9in. wide. $2,250 £1,000

Victorian inlaid figured walnut piano front Davenport desk, 23in. wide. $2,250 £1,000

Davenport in rosewood with baluster gallery and sphinx-carved cupports. $3,600 £1,600

DISPLAY CABINETS

Late 19th century mahogany display cabinet.
$160 £70

Edwardian mahogany china cabinet enclosed by three glazed doors, 4ft.6in. wide.
$285 £125

Small Edwardian inlaid mahogany display cabinet.
$340 £150

19th century mahogany display table with brass embellishments. $450 £200

Small walnut cabinet with gilt mounts, 30in. wide.
$605 £270

Mahogany display cabinet, circa 1910, 48in. wide.
$675 £300

Mahogany display cabinet, 1890's, 79 x 36in.
$765 £340

Mahogany vitrine, circa 1895, 68in. high.
$845 £375

Late 19th century Continental mahogany display cabinet of polygonal form, 80cm. wide. $855 £380

58

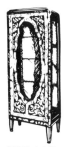

Early 1920's Art Deco walnut and giltwood vitrine, 172cm. high. $990 £440

Mahogany vitrine, 34 x 17in., 1880-1900. $1,080 £480

Edwardian mahogany framed display cabinet with shaped mirrored pediment. $1,080 £480

Mahogany and marquetry display cabinet, 1900's, 49in. wide. $1,285 £570

Edwardian inlaid and banded mahogany bow-fronted corner display cabinet, 33in. wide. $1,405 £625

Biedermeier fruitwood display cabinet, 50½in. wide. $1,530 £680

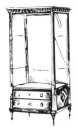

Early 19th century mahogany vitrine, frieze with gilt bronze banding, 36in. wide. $1,620 £720

Chippendale mahogany display cabinet with a blind fret cornice, 57in. wide, circa 1890. $1,915 £850

Art Nouveau display cabinet with leaded glazing. $1,970 £875

DISPLAY CABINETS

Austrian display cabinet, circa 1900-1910, 120.5cm. wide.
$2,025 £900

Edwardian rosewood and marquetry display cabinet with two drawers.
$2,050 £910

Mid 19th century Flemish carved oak display cabinet, 41½in. wide.
$2,070 £920

Dutch marquetry display cabinet, circa 1840, 55in. wide.
$2,475 £1,100

Late 19th century satinwood and inlaid shaped fronted display cabinet, 123cm. wide.
$3,040 £1,350

Mahogany cabinet by Louis Majorelle, circa 1900, 30½in. wide.
$3,150 £1,400

Early 20th century serpentine marquetry vitrine with brown marble top, 31½in. wide.
$3,375 £1,500

One of a pair of unusual 19th century satinwood china display cabinets, 14in. wide.
$4,050 £1,800

19th century Chinese hardwood display cabinet.
$4,950 £2,200

19th century French rose-wood and Vernis Martin vitrine, 57in. wide, with ormolu mounts.
$4,950 £2,200

Early display cabinet by Charles Mackintosh, circa 1895.
$6,190 £2,750

Dutch walnut and marque-try display cabinet with arched top, circa 1840, 87in. high.$6,525 £2,900

Mahogany framed circular display cabinet on stand with scrolling legs, circa 1900. $7,200 £3,200

19th century Japanese Shibayama display cabinet.
$9,000 £4,000

19th century French king-wood vitrine, door panels painted in the Vernis Martin manner.
$9,450 £4,200

Louis XV style kingwood display and writing cabinet, circa 1860.$11,250 £5,000

One of a pair of tulipwood display cabinets with arched upper parts, circa 1900, 31½in. wide.
$12,375 £5,500

Mid 19th century Dutch mar-quetry display cabinet, 4ft. 9in. wide. $30,375 £13,500

61

DRESSERS

Small Victorian stripped pine dresser base with shaped brass handles, 4ft. wide. $315 £140

19th century German dresser with two drawers.
                    $315 £140

A carved oak dresser, the drawers in the frieze with carved lion mask handles, 4ft. wide. $450 £200

Early 20th century oak dresser with brass handles.
          $565 £250

Victorian carved oak dresser with pot board. $565 £250

Late Victorian pine dresser. $565 £250

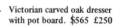

19th century Jacobean style dresser, 4ft.7in. wide.
          $675 £300

Late 19th century walnut Continental dresser.
          $675 £300

Small 19th century stripped pine dresser with drawers and cupboards, 3ft.3in. wide. $785 £350

Continental cupboard dresser, 47in. wide, circa 1840. $810 £360

Oak dresser with split baluster decoration, circa 1860, 59in. wide. $1,070 £475

Victorian mahogany dresser with brass fittings. $1,070 £475

Mahogany buffet, circa 1895, 64in. high. $1,125 £500

Victorian 'Dog Kennel' dresser, circa 1850, 63in. wide. $1,295 £575

Early 19th century stripped pine dresser with pot board. $1,350 £600

Early 19th century dresser and rack in honey coloured oak, 64in. wide. $1,800 £800

Early 19th century oak dresser with raised plate rack, 5ft.7in. wide. $2,925 £1,300

Art Nouveau walnut buffet, English, circa 1900, 68½in. wide. $3,150 £1,400

A small Edwardian mahogany serving table on a tripod base. $225 £100

Victorian walnut dumb waiter of two circular tiers, 1ft.8in. diam. $270 £120

19th century two-tier dumb waiter with turned central column, 68cm. diam. $630 £280

William IV period mahogany dumb waiter of three shelves, 42in. high. $790 £350

19th century two-tier dumb waiter with marquetry and ormolu mounts. $790 £350

19th century mahogany three-tier dumb waiter of Georgian design, 118cm. high. $790 £350

Regency mahogany three-tier dumb waiter with revolving shelves, 29in. wide. $810 £360

Regency period two-tier dumb waiter on splay feet with castors. $1,015 £450

Regency mahogany dumb waiter with brass gallery and reeded tripod base with claw castors. $1,350 £600

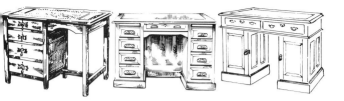

Late 19th century mahogany desk with tooled leather top. $115 £50

Early 20th century oak kneehole desk with inset leather top. $450 £200

Mid 19th century mahogany pedestal desk, 36in. wide. $450 £200

Mahogany pedestal desk with leather top, 4ft.6in. wide, circa 1900. $565 £250

Late Georgian mahogany gentleman's kneehole desk, circa 1830, 36in. wide. $600 £265

Late 19th century shaped front kneehole writing desk on splay feet. $645 £285

Late 19th century oak pedestal desk with seventeen drawers, 168cm. wide. $675 £300

Carved oak writing desk, circa 1880, 51½in. wide. $675 £300

Victorian mahogany cylinder pedestal desk. $990 £440

Mid 19th century carved oak pedestal desk, top with outset corners, 62in. wide. $1,080 £480

Rosewood kneehole specimen cabinet, 1840's, 58in. wide. $1,080 £480

19th century Oriental carved teak writing desk. $990 £440

Small oak kneehole desk with cupboard doors, 45in. wide. $1,125 £500

Walnut desk inlaid with various woods by Daneway, circa 1910. $1,125 £500

Early 20th century oak roll-top desk with fitted interior. $1,240 £550

Seddon style carved oak and decorated kneehole desk, circa 1860. $1,350 £600

19th century secretaire kneehole desk in mahogany, 3ft.1in. wide. $1,350 £600

19th century japanned pedestal desk, 3ft.10in. long. $1,465 £650

Early 20th century maho-
gany pedestal cylinder desk,
54½in. wide. $1,520 £675

Carved walnut pedestal
desk, 1860's, 46in. wide.
$1,620 £720

Early 19th century ebon-
ised pedestal desk decorated
with brass moulding, circa
1820. $1,690 £750

Early 20th century Chinese
pedestal desk.
$3,265 £1,450

19th century walnut and
kingwood, kidney-shaped
kneehole desk, the top
lined with tooled leather.
$4,500 £2,000

Late George III mahogany
pedestal desk, circa 1810,
4ft.4in. wide.
$6,300 £2,800

'Louis XIV' boulle bureau
mazarin, 48in. wide, circa
1850. $8,550 £3,800

Victorian oak pedestal
desk by Thomas Knight.
$9,450 £4,200

Early 19th century ivory
inlaid kneehole desk, 3ft.
5in. wide.$22,500 £10,000

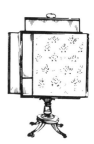

Late 19th century brass and glass firescreen. $65 £30

Mid 19th century brass pole with beadwork screen, supported on ebonised base. $200 £90

Mahogany framed three-panel extending screen. $215 £95

Large light rosewood wool-work firescreen, 1850's, 53 x 38½in. $295 £130

Walnut pole screen with circular embroidered panel, 60in. high, circa 1860. $400 £180

John Pearson bronze and wrought iron firescreen, circa 1906, 27½in. high. $450 £200

Late 19th century Damascus Mishrabaya hardwood three-fold screen, 78in. high. $620 £275

Victorian parlour firescreen, 4ft. high, in double-glazed glass case. $700 £310

Mahogany and leather five-fold screen, circa 1900, 85in. wide. $790 £350

Three-fold painted screen, circa 1910, panel signed Jules Vernon-Fair.
$955 £425

Giltwood and stained glass screen, circa 1900, 62in. wide. $1,015 £450

19th century Chinese hardwood screen with red and black lacquer. $1,150 £510

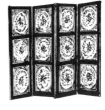

Kingwood, tulipwood and mahogany three-fold screen, circa 1900, 76in. high.
$1,170 £520

Late 19th century ivory, mother-of-pearl and Shibayama two-fold screen, 64in. high. $2,475 £1,100

Walnut four-fold screen inset with oval embroidered reserves, 76in. tall, circa 1860. $3,600 £1,600

American lead glass firescreen, circa 1900, 45¼in. high. $3,825 £1,700

19th century Oriental padouk four-fold screen, 228cm. wide.
$4,165 £1,850

Early 19th century six-leaf screen, 70½in. high.
$6,750 £3,000

Victorian rosewood secretaire Wellington chest. $745 £330

Regency mahogany secretaire chest with ebony stringing. $900 £400

South German mahogany secretaire, 1840's, 39in. wide. $955 £425

Burr-chestnut secretaire semanier with white marble top, 1870's, 26in. wide. $1,015 £450

Georgian mahogany fall-front secretaire, circa 1835. $1,015 £450

Victorian oak secretaire cabinet, 36in. wide. $1,465 £650

19th century coromandel wood chest with a fitted secretaire drawer. $1,575 £700

George IV mahogany secretaire cabinet, circa 1825, 3ft.6½in. wide. $1,575 £700

A teak secretaire military chest, 30in. wide, circa 1820. $1,690 £750

Charles X mahogany secretaire, circa 1830, 3ft.3in. wide. $1,690 £750

French 19th century floral marquetry escritoire in walnut and kingwood. $1,750 £775

Biedermeier mahogany secretaire, 3ft.9in. wide, circa 1820-40. $1,800 £800

Early 19th century Dutch mahogany secretaire. $3,940 £1,750

Satinwood secretaire a abattant, possibly Polish, circa 1820, 2ft.10in. wide. $4,500 £2,000

Oak secretaire by M. H. Baillie-Scott with pewter and marquetry inlay, 46in. high. $4,950 £2,200

Serpentine kingwood and marquetry secretaire, circa 1870, 27½in. wide. $5,965 £2,650

19th century satinwood escritoire, 95cm. wide. $7,200 £3,200

Empire ormolu mounted mahogany secretaire a abattant, circa 1810, 3ft. 2¼in. wide. $10,125 £4,500

71

SECRETAIRE BOOKCASES

American mahogany secretaire, 40in. wide, circa 1860-80. $425 £190

Late 19th century walnut secretaire bookcase. $745 £330

Satinwood secretaire with scalloped gallery, circa 1900, 27½in. wide. $945 £420

19th century Burmese carved hardwood secretaire cabinet. $1,170 £520

Victorian mahogany secretaire bookcase on turned legs. $1,685 £750

Early 19th century mahogany secretaire bookcase with satinwood interior, 3ft.9in. wide. $1,825 £810

Dutch mahogany secretaire bookcase with carved cresting, late 1840's, 40½in. wide. $2,205 £980

Early 19th century American mahogany writing cabinet, 4ft.2in. wide. $2,250 £1,000

American figured mahogany and satinwood lined cylinder secretaire bookcase, 4ft.1in. wide. $2,925 £1,300

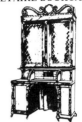

Secretaire bookcase of late Regency period, with lattice glazed doors of unusual design. $3,150 £1,400

Late Georgian secretaire bookcase in mahogany with astragal glazed doors. $3,490 £1,550

Mahogany secretaire bookcase with gilt enrichments, possibly Irish, circa 1835, 258cm. high. $4,050 £1,800

Regency secretaire military cabinet in burr-elm, circa 1820. $4,500 £2,000

Regency mahogany breakfront secretaire bookcase, 185cm. wide. $4,500 £2,000

George III mahogany secretaire chest, 42in. wide. $6,750 £3,000

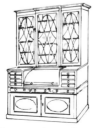

Regency mahogany breakfront secretaire bookcase, 84in. wide. $8,440 £3,750

Regency mahogany bureau cabinet with tambour cylinder cover, 4ft.4½in. wide. $10,350 £4,600

George IV mahogany breakfront secretaire bookcase by Gillow. $16,875 £7,500

73

SETTEES & COUCHES

20th century oak monk's bench.
$180 £80

Cast iron and wooden slatted garden seat.
$180 £80

Edwardian inlaid mahogany couch on cabriole legs. $450 £200

Mid 19th century grained rosewood chaise longue. $450 £200

Late 19th century oak settle, 49¾in. wide.
$450 £200

Ash settle designed for Liberty & Co., circa 1900, 51in. wide.
$495 £220

19th century carved walnut twin chair-back settee. $495 £220

Early 19th century Indian hardwood palanquin, 4ft.4in. wide. $495 £220

Victorian mahogany scroll end settee on turned legs.
$495 £220

Mahogany and marquetry settee, circa 1900, 51½in. wide.
$520 £230

Scottish 'William IV' chaise longue with moulded frame and overscrolled ends, late 1830's, 78in.
$630 £280

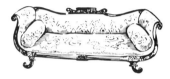

Regency couch in mahogany inlaid with ormolu.
$675 £300

Regency painted settee, circa 1805, 6ft. 11in. wide.
$820 £365

A carved oak hall settle, 56in. long.
$900 £400

Mid 19th century ebonised settee with button upholstered back and seat, 68in. wide, probably German.
$945 £420

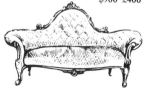

Walnut settee, 75in. long, circa 1860, with carved toprail.
$990 £440

75

Chippendale mahogany chair-back settee, circa 1880-1900, 72in. wide. $990 £440

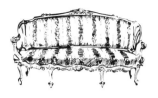

Early 20th century 'Louis XV' giltwood canape, 72½in. wide. $1,015 £450

Burmese settee of serpentine shape extensively carved and pierced. $1,015 £450

Satinwood settee with double panel back and curved arms, 46in. wide. $1,035 £460

Giltwood Duchesse, circa 1880, on cabriole legs with scroll feet. $1,080 £480

English walnut chaise longue, with button upholstered end and half back, circa 1860, 74¾in. long. $1,080 £480

Victorian walnut framed serpentine shaped settee, 183cm. wide. $1,188 £528

George IV mahogany settee, circa 1820, 6ft.1in. long. $1,395 £620

Carved giltwood day bed with ribbon carved frame, circa 1880, 88in. wide. $1,465 £650

Mid 19th century Dutch mahogany and marquetry settee of three sections, 65in. wide. $1,575 £700

Early 19th century couch of classical form, 6ft. long. $1,690 £750

Late 19th century mother-of-pearl inlaid hardwood settee, circa 1880, 6ft.7in. long. $1,915 £850

Italian parcel gilt mahogany chaise longue, circa 1815, 5ft.9in. long. $2,225 £990

19th century ornate carved oak settle in French Renaissance style, 195cm. wide. $2,475 £1,100

Upholstered swing seat, 90in. tall, circa 1880, made in India. $2,925 £1,300

Russian amboyna wood chaise longue with gilt enrichments. $15,750 £7,000

Victorian stripped pine hanging shelves. $45 £20

Stained beech and composition corner bracket, 30in. high, circa 1880. $115 £50

Set of stripped pine hanging bookshelves, George III period, 38in. long. $126 £56

Mahogany Regency set of hanging shelves with carved cresting, circa 1820, 26½in. wide. $215 £95

19th century mahogany 'Chinese Chippendale' style three-tier wall shelf with fretwork gallery, 56cm. wide. $295 £130

One of a pair of mahogany corner shelves, mid 19th century, 34in. high. $630 £280

One of a pair of late 19th century mahogany hanging shelves, 36¼in. wide. $720 £320

One of a pair of early 20th century giltwood mirror shelves, 42in. high. $1,125 £500

One of a pair of Regency mahogany standing bookshelves, circa 1810, 2ft. 6½in. wide. $5,175 £2,300

Small 20th century Jacobean style oak sideboard. $100 £45

Art Deco sideboard in amboyna wood, 5ft.2in. long. $170 £75

Victorian carved oak sideboard with brass fittings. $170 £75

Victorian mahogany sideboard with cellarette drawer. $340 £150

Custom mahogany Jacobean style sideboard with carved gallery, 58in. wide. $385 £170

Small sideboard in pale walnut, 1930's, 136.5cm. wide. $450 £200

Mid 19th century rosewood sideboard, 68 x 66in. $450 £200

Late 19th century carved oak sideboard with brass fittings. $450 £200

19th century inlaid mahogany sideboard with brass gallery. $450 £200

SIDEBOARDS

Edwardian mahogany sideboard with five drawers. $475 £210

Stained oak sideboard, circa 1880, 56in. wide. $520 £230

Olivewood breakfront sideboard with two central cupboard doors, 72in. wide, circa 1930. $630 £280

Small English ebonised mahogany sideboard. $730 £325

A walnut and burr-walnut open sideboard, the canted corners held by female caryatids, 58in. wide, circa 1850. $675 £300

Regency mahogany sideboard, richly veneered, 4ft.9in. wide. $790 £350

Early Victorian mahogany sideboard, mirror back carved with acanthus, fruit and 'C' scrolls, 84½in. wide. $855 £380

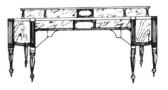

A large, Regency, crossbanded mahogany sideboard on turned legs. $900 £400

19th century painted satinwood sideboard. $1,070 £475

Early 19th century mahogany sideboard on tapered legs with spade feet. $1,090 £485

Gillow & Co. mahogany sideboard, 190cm. wide, 1880's. $1,280 £570

William IV mahogany and crossbanded bow-front sideboard, 155cm. wide. $1,350 £600

Mid 19th century oak sideboard, heavily carved, 90in. wide. $2,025 £900

Late Georgian mahogany bow-fronted small sideboard. $2,700 £1,200

Large carved oak sideboard, 19th century, Flemish, 8ft.2in. long. $6,190 £2,750

Ebonised sideboard with silver-plated mounts, about 1875. $18,000 £8,000

81

Victorian mahogany towel
rail on twist supports.

20th century oak umbrella
stand. $35 £15

$45 £20

20th century mahogany folding cake stand. $55 £25

Late 19th century bentwood
hat stand. $115 £50

Late 19th century oak hall
stand with brass fittings.
$170 £75

Late 19th century mahogany
shaving stand. $225 £100

Victorian mahogany hat
stand in the Gothic manner.
$225 £100

Oriental hardwood marble
topped stand. $250 £110

Mid 19th century walnut
music stand with double
rests. $315 £140

Marquetry jardiniere, circa 1890, 31 x 27in.
$450 £200

One of a pair of Italian ebony and majolica plant stands.
$520 £230

19th century mahogany music stand with hinged easel, 52cm. wide.
$630 £280

Late 19th century walnut urn stand, 22½in. high.
$765 £340

Heavily carved oak hall stand with lifting lidded seat. $835 £370

Regency William IV double music stand in rosewood.
$900 £400

One of a pair of red and green tortoiseshell boulle centre pedestals, circa 1830. $1,035 £460

Early Victorian mahogany folio rack. $1,240 £550

Two-tiered rosewood jardiniere stand, circa 1895, 16in. square.
$1,880 £835

Late 19th century elm stool. $35 £15

19th century Georgian style mahogany stool on shaped legs. $55 £25

Late 19th century oak joint stool. $65 £30

Late 19th century Oriental carved teak stool. $65 £30

Late 19th century oak piano stool with cane-work seat. $65 £30

George III style dressing stool with needlework top, 45cm. wide. $90 £40

Victorian walnut stool with original castors, circa 1850. $100 £45

Late 19th century mahogany piano stool on carved cabriole legs. $125 £55

Victorian wind-up piano stool, upholstered in Dralon. $135 £60

A Danish marquetry stool,
2ft.3in. wide, circa 1820.
$340 £150

Renouvin Art Deco music
stool, 78.25cm. wide.
$395 £175

Second Empire mahogany
stool with drop-in seat,
19½in. square, circa 1870.
$765 £340

Early Victorian rosewood,
gros point stool.
$785 £350

Stained walnut stool, circa
1890, 43in. high.
$2,250 £1,000

Egyptian carved walnut
stool, circa 1920.
$2,590 £1,150

A mid 19th century brass
X-frame stool, 2ft.5in.
wide. $3,375 £1,500

Early 19th century window
seat in the manner of
Duncan Phyfe.
$3,940 £1,750

Regency mahogany and
parcel gilt stool, circa 1810,
1ft.10½in. wide.
$5,175 £2,300

Suite of tubular chromed metal cantilever seat furniture, 1930's, 80cm.
$450 £200

Elmwood spindle back cottage suite in excellent condition. $595 £265

Part of an Art Deco drawingroom suite, late 1930's, upholstered in velvet.
$900 £400

English cast iron seat with two chairs decorated in the fern pattern, about 1870
80, seat 4ft.6in. wide, chair 2ft. wide.
$900 £400

Part of an Edwardian mahogany five-piece suite. $1,035 £460

A mahogany inlaid and satinwood banded drawingroom suite with pierced trellis splats, on turned legs, comprising an arm settee, two armchairs and four single chairs. $1,125 £500

Three-piece Victorian suite with scalloped crests and turned trumpet form front supports. $1,465 £650

Button upholstered walnut drawingroom suite, 1860's. $1,935 £860

SUITES

Part of an Edwardian inlaid seven-piece mahogany suite. $2,250 £1,000

A mid Victorian period suite, comprising settee, grandfather chair and grandmother chair, inlaid with ebony and amboyna wood. $2,250 £1,000

Part of a late 19th century walnut nine-piece suite with upholstered seats and backs. $3,150 £1,400

Lacquered three-piece bergere suite, framework painted with chinoiserie, circa 1920. $3,490 £1,550

Part of a Victorian nine-piece suite in walnut. $5,400 £2,400

Part of a suite of Louis XVI giltwood seat furniture of five pieces, circa 1880.
$8,100 £3,600

Liberty & Co. inlaid oak bedroom suite, circa 1900. $9,900 £4,400

A Victorian suite of sofa and two chairs in rosewood with velvet upholstery.
$51,750 £23,000

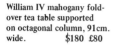

William IV mahogany fold-over tea table supported on octagonal column, 91cm. wide. $180 £80

19th century mahogany fold-over card table in the Chippendale style, 89cm. wide. $270 £120

19th century inlaid mahogany and flap-over card table. $360 £160

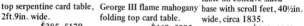

Victorian walnut swivel top serpentine card table, 2ft.9in. wide. $385 £170

George III flame mahogany folding top card table. $460 £205

William IV mahogany tea table on concave sided base with scroll feet, 40½in. wide, circa 1835. $540 £240

Rosewood card table, 1840's, 36in. wide. $540 £240

Antique oak tea table on cabriole legs, circa 1840, 35in. wide. $620 £275

Edwardian mahogany envelope table with floral marquetry decoration, 57cm. wide. $630 £280

Burr-walnut card table, 1860's, 35in. wide. $700 £310

Late 19th century English walnut card table on moulded cabriole legs, 33¾in. wide. $700 £310

Victorian burr-walnut folding top card table on cabriole legs. $730 £325

Edwardian inlaid rosewood envelope card table. $765 £340

19th century mahogany fold-over top card table. $845 £375

Victorian rosewood fold-over card table. $865 £385

Georgian walnut fold-over card table with protruding corners. $875 £390

Dutch marquetry and mahogany serpentine fronted card table, circa 1880, 2ft.4in. wide. $945 £420

Regency brass inlaid burr-elm card table, circa 1820, 3ft.2in. wide. $945 £420

Regency brass inlaid rosewood card table, 2ft.11½in. wide, circa 1810.
$1,350 £600

George IV satinwood card table, circa 1825, 3ft. wide. $1,485 £660

Kingwood card table with brass bound rim, 31in. square, circa 1880.
$1,575 £700

Boulle card table, circa 1860, inlaid with cut brass foliage on a red tortoiseshell ground.
$1,575 £700

French Empire rosewood and walnut folding top card table, 2ft.9½in. wide. $1,685 £750

19th century marquetry and kingwood swivel top card table. $2,475 £1,100

Regency rosewood tea table on four concave shaped legs, 2ft.11½in. wide. $2,700 £1,200

Regency brass inlaid card table, circa 1815, 2ft.11½in. wide, in mahogany with rosewood crossbanding.
$2,925 £1,300

One of a pair of mid 19th century English folding card tables.
$12,375 £5,500

Victorian cast iron consol table with marble top. $280 £125

Wood and perspex consol table, 1930's, 91.25cm. high. $450 £200

William IV consol table in rosewood, 3ft.2in. wide. $1,015 £450

Marble top mahogany consol table with D-shaped centre frieze, circa 1900, 70in. wide. $1,125 £500

Mid 19th century rosewood consol table, one of a pair, 48in. wide. $1,125 £500

One of a pair of painted D-shaped consol tables with satinwood banding, circa 1870. $3,150 £1,400

Fine lacquered wood and chrome consol table by D. Desky, circa 1927, 72in. wide. $5,625 £2,500

One of a pair of Empire ormolu mounted bronze and mahogany consols, 1ft.6in. wide. $5,625 £2,500

Regency giltwood consol table with Sicilian jasper top, 35¾in. wide. $7,200 £3,200

DINING TABLES

20th century oak draw-leaf table on twist supports. $65 £30

19th century mahogany snap-top table on tripod base. $190 £85

Victorian mahogany centre table, 3ft. wide, on cabriole legs. $370 £165

Walnut centre table, circa 1870, 48½in. wide. $450 £200

Small Victorian mahogany centre table on a platform base with claw feet. $450 £200

Walnut breakfast table, circa 1860, 53½in. wide. $640 £285

Round walnut dining table with carved legs and stretchers, sold with six matching chairs. $665 £295

Victorian mahogany centre table on quadruple base. $745 £330

Mahogany breakfast table, 4ft.6in. x 3ft.6in. $790 £350

94

Circular rosewood Oriental carved table. $810 £360

Burr-walnut circular breakfast table, 1860's, 48in. diam. $1,125 £500

Rosewood circular breakfast table, 64in. diam., 1830's. $1,170 £520

Mid 19th century Batavian ebony centre table, 47in. diam. $1,390 £620

19th century coromandel breakfast table, 4ft. diam. $1,620 £720

Mahogany drum table, circa 1840, 3ft.10in. diam. $1,635 £725

North German or Russian mahogany centre table, circa 1820, 2ft.6½in. square. $2,025 £900

19th century scarlet boulle and ebonised centre table. $2,140 £950

Regency mahogany centre table, circa 1815, 4ft.1in. diam. $2,475 £1,100

95

Regency mahogany drum table with circular leather top, 46in. wide.
$2,925 £1,300

Regency period rosewood circular snap-top breakfast table, 4ft. diam.
$3,600 £1,600

Victorian inlaid walnut table with carved scrolled supports and legs.
$3,825 £1,700

Regency zebra wood breakfast table with mahogany crossbanding, 4ft.8in. x 3ft.6in. $5,625 £2,500

George III mahogany breakfast table with tip-up top, 60in. wide. $6,075 £2,700

Circular Victorian tilt-top table in walnut marquetry.
$6,300 £2,800

Regency rosewood breakfast table with brass inlaid banding, early 19th century, by John Keene.
$6,525 £2,900

Early Victorian marquetry centre table, 64in. diam., circa 1840.$8,440 £3,750

Large George III mahogany breakfast table, 5ft. diam., circa 1800.$9,000 £4,000

Victorian mahogany dressing table. $315 £140

19th century Sheraton style satinwood veneered dressing table, 21in. wide. $330 £145

Liberty & Co. oak toilet table, 38½in. wide, circa 1900. $395 £175

High Kitsch dressing table, 161cm. high, 1930's. $640 £285

Mid 19th century walnut and ormolu mounted toilet table, signed Tahn of Paris, 53cm. wide. $1,240 £550

George III mahogany dressing table by Gillow of Lancaster, circa 1805, 3ft.6in. wide. $2,025 £900

Early Victorian bird's eye maple and marquetry kneehole dressing table and matching toilet mirror, 60in. wide. $3,940 £1,750

Empire mahogany dressing table with arched swing mirror, 30in. wide. $4,050 £1,800

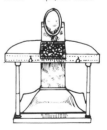

Dressing table by Emile-Jacques Ruhlmann, circa 1920, 43½in. wide. $20,250 £9,000

97

Late 19th century beech-wood Sutherland table on turned legs. $45 £20

Late Victorian stripped pine Pembroke table with drawer, on turned legs. $165 £75

A rosewood inlaid oblong two-tier table with folding leaves and satinwood banded borders, 2ft. wide. $225 £100

Victorian carved oak gate-leg table on barley twist supports. $225 £100

Country made oak drop-leaf table, circa 1820. $225 £100

George III mahogany Pembroke table crossbanded in satinwood, 114cm. wide. $295 £130

19th century solid mahogany Sutherland table on turned legs. $340 £150

19th century mahogany drop-flap table on pad feet. $340 £150

Walnut veneered Victorian Sutherland table. $565 £250

Early 19th century mahogany breakfast table on quadruple sabre leg base. $790 £350

19th century mahogany Wake's table with double gateleg action.$900 £400

Regency mahogany breakfast table with a detachable leaf. $1,015 £450

Italian parquetry top oak and walnut writing table, 105cm. wide. $1,035 £460

George III mahogany dining table, circa 1810. $1,125 £500

Mahogany Pembroke table on reeded legs, circa 1800. $1,125 £500

William IV mahogany dining table, 1830's, 48in. wide. $1,690 £750

19th century satinwood Pembroke table, 32½in. wide. $1,690 £750

Regency mahogany extending dining table, circa 1815, 8ft.4in. long.$3,220 £1,430

LARGE TABLES

20th century oak reproduction refectory table. $495 £220

William IV rosewood library table, 1830's, 54in. wide. $520 £230

Walnut centre table, circa 1860, 48in. wide. $540 £240

Mid 19th century American pitch pine refectory table, 96½in. long. $745 £330

Mahogany dining table, circa 1920's, 96in. long, extended. $790 £350

20th century mahogany dining table with marble top, 58in. wide.
                                        $820 £365

Mid 19th century mahogany expanding dining table, on ten turned legs.
                                        $1,035 £460

Large oak refectory table, 1880's, 108in. long. $1,295 £575

Mid 19th century mahogany centre table, 51½in. wide. $1,440 £640

Carved rosewood library table.
$1,465 £650

Mid 19th century walnut centre table, 72in. long. $1,630 £725

Solid mahogany dining table which makes two breakfast tables, circa 1830.
$1,690 £750

Mahogany dining table with lattice under-framing, George IV, circa 1825, 7ft.6in. x 4ft.5in. $1,915 £850

Early 19th century mahogany pedestal dining table, extending to 12ft., with extra pedestal. $3,600 £1,600

George III mahogany three pedestal dining table, 51 x 152in. extended.
$4,500 £2,000

Thurston full size billiard table, 1907, 151 x 80in. $22,500 £10,000

OCCASIONAL TABLES

Victorian bamboo occasional table with lacquered top. $56 £25

19th century mahogany occasional table on tripod base. $100 £45

Late 19th century carved oak triangular top table with flaps. $135 £60

19th century Burmese teak occasional table, legs in the form of elephants' heads. $135 £60

Victorian walnut circular occasional table on a carved tripod base. $170 £75

19th century lacquered nest of tables. $215 £95

Early 1920's marble topped Art Deco occasional table, 54.5cm. square.$250 £110

Mid 19th century French marquetry side table of kingwood, 54cm. wide. $270 £120

19th century rosewood centre table on a stretcher base. $295 £130

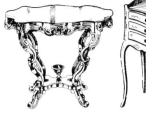

Victorian walnut turtle top table with white marble top. $300 £135

Syrie Maugham painted wood occasional table, circa 1936, 66.5cm. high. $325 £145

Louis XV style two-tier etagere with floral marquetry, 74cm. wide. $400 £180

Rosewood and marquetry occasional table, late 19th century, 18¼in. wide. $400 £180

English rosewood serpentine top centre table on cabriole legs, circa 1840, 49in. wide. $400 £180

19th century mahogany galleried table. $460 £205

Late 19th century mahogany vide poche, 1ft.6in. wide. $495 £220

Hardwood camel, 28in. high, which supports a carved coffee table. $540 £240

Victorian walnut table with round marble top inlaid with intricate patterns. $565 £250

A Galle oak and marquetry etagere, the shaped rectangular top inlaid in various printwoods. $650 £290

Rosewood and parquetry specimen table, circa 1850. $675 £300

Mahogany display table, circa 1890, 33in. high. $730 £325

French mahogany centre table, circa 1900, 36in. wide. $730 £325

Octagonal walnut inlaid table, circa 1840, 28in. high. $745 £330

Ebonised and marquetry occasional table, 1880's, 44in. wide. $900 £400

Regency rosewood centre table with circular top, 24in. diam., inset with 18th century Imari dish. $955 £425

19th century walnut, kingwood and tulipwood serpentine top centre table, 3ft.3½in. wide. $1,125 £500

Mid 19th century Italian ebonised blackamoor table with marble top, 20½in. diam. $1,485 £660

Boulle jardiniere with zinc container on cabriole legs, 1860's, 31½in. wide.
$1,620 £720

Early 20th century 'Louis XV' giltwood pier table with red marble top, 50in. wide. $2,070 £920

Marquetry centre table, circa 1870, 62in. wide, by H. Goodall, Newcastle.
$2,590 £1,150

One of a pair of North Italian kingwood D-shaped bedside cupboards, 1ft. 10in. wide. $2,700 £1,200

Set of four marquetry tables with glass tops, circa 1900, by Galle.
$2,925 £1,300

Rosewood coffee table by Jacques Rhulmann, circa 1925, 26½in. diam.
$3,825 £1,700

Kingwood and Sevres etagere, top inset with porcelain dish, 1870's, 29in. high. $4,725 £2,100

Louis XVI design kingwood and purple-heart centre table by Joubert, 1814, 36½in. wide. $5,625 £2,500

Dutch marquetry centre table, circa 1830, with late 17th century panels.
$10,125 £4,500

20th century oak side table. $80 £35

Late Victorian walnut side table with undershelf. $170 £75

Oak side table, 1880's, 28 x 43in. $330 £145

Art Deco side table, 137cm. wide, 1930's. $540 £240

20th century mahogany side table, 57in. wide. $565 £250

Stained oak side table, circa 1880, 38in. wide. $565 £250

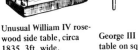

A 19th century carved rosewood side table. $745 £330

Unusual William IV rosewood side table, circa 1835, 3ft. wide. $745 £330

George III mahogany side table on square tapering legs, 34in. high. $845 £375

19th century French rosewood side table with D-ends. $1,350 £600

Regency rosewood pier table in the manner of Thomas Hope, 46½in. wide. $1,575 £700

19th century boulle side table with ormolu mounts. $1,690 £750

19th century Dutch floral marquetry walnut side table. $1,800 £800

Late George III mahogany bow-fronted side table, 2ft.11in. wide, circa 1805. $2,250 £1,000

Regency rosewood and satinwood band inlaid side table. $2,250 £1,000

Shagreen covered side table, 1920's, 40cm. high. $2,925 £1,300

One of a pair of Regency side tables, 23in. high. $12,375 £5,500

Thomas Hope gilt pier table with black marble slab. $27,000 £12,000

Mahogany sofa table, circa 1840, 54in. wide.
$500 £225

William IV rosewood sofa table, 88cm. wide.
$845 £375

Early 19th century mahogany sofa table with two end drawers. $855 £380

Regency mahogany sofa table, circa 1815, 5ft. 10in. wide. $990 £440

Edwardian mahogany sofa table, 58in. wide.
$1,010 £450

Regency rosewood sofa table with satinwood inlaid top, 26in. wide.
$1,125 £500

Early 19th century Anglo-Indian ebony sofa table, 4ft.2in. wide.
$1,125 £500

Mahogany and marquetry sofa table, circa 1890, 44in. wide. $1,215 £540

Regency mahogany pedestal sofa table, 59in. wide open. $1,440 £640

19th century Dutch mahogany and satinwood crossbanded sofa table, 42in. wide. $1,690 £720

Regency brass inlaid rosewood sofa table, circa 1815, 3ft.7in. wide. $3,095 £1,375

Regency rosewood and brass strung sofa table on four sabre legs on platform base. $3,220 £1,430

Dutch marquetry and mahogany sofa table, circa 1820, 4ft.2in. wide. $3,375 £1,500

Regency mahogany sofa table, 5ft. wide open, circa 1810. $3,600 £1,600

Regency brass inlaid sofa table in rosewood. $4,500 £2,000

Regency rosewood sofa table/games table with satinwood crossbanded top. $5,445 £2,420

Early 19th century black lacquer table, 38in. wide closed. $5,850 £2,600

One of a pair of Regency rosewood sofa tables by John McLean, 2ft. deep. $24,750 £11,000

Victorian games table in mahogany on a central column with platform base. $225 £100

19th century mahogany workbox on platform base. $300 £135

Victorian rosewood work table with sliding bag. $340 £150

Victorian walnut veneered work table, dated 1889, 22¾in. wide. $400 £180

Rosewood work table, circa 1850, 30 x 22½in. $430 £190

19th century burr-walnut work table with diamond inlay top, 61cm. wide. $450 £200

Mid 19th century Chinese export lacquer work sewing table on paw feet. $475 £210

19th century pollard elm work table with brass claw castors. $505 £225

Anglo-Indian ebony games table, 30 x 22in. $540 £240

Early Victorian sewing table with drop flaps and a U-shaped centre support.
$565 £250

William IV brass inlaid rosewood chess table, 1ft. 9in. wide, circa 1830.
$620 £275

A lady's small mahogany combined writing desk and work table, circa 1900.
$640 £285

Victorian rosewood needle-work table. $655 £290

19th century marquetry work table on fine turned legs. $675 £300

English walnut combined work and games table with divided swivelling top, 1850's, 28in. high.
$675 £300

Mahogany and marquetry sewing cabinet with a gallery top, circa 1900.
$720 £320

Victorian fitted burr-walnut work table.
$745 £330

Floral marquetry Irish yew-wood sewing table.
$790 £350

111

English walnut and marquetry lady's work table, circa 1850, 28in. high. $810 £360

Mid 19th century ebony sewing table, 25in. high. $845 £375

Late Regency walnut and rosewood work table inlaid with brass, copper and mother-of-pearl, 21in. wide. $900 £400

Victorian papier mache octagonal work table inlaid with mother-of-pearl, 47cm. wide. $900 £400

Early 19th century combined games and sewing table in rosewood. $955 £425

Victorian rosewood and crossbanded chess top work table, inlaid with floral marquetry. $990 £440

20th century Carine parquetry games table, 37in. wide. $1,010 £450

Walnut combined work and games table, 1860's, 33¼in. wide. $1,010 £450

Ayres mahogany 'racing roulette' games table, circa 1900, 173cm. long. $1,240 £550

Chinese export black and gilt lacquer games table, circa 1850, 35in. wide. $1,240 £550

George IV boulle games table, circa 1830, 1ft.6in. wide. $1,350 £600

Regency mahogany games table complete with playing pieces. $1,350 £600

Marquetry walnut work table with serpentine top, circa 1870, 20¾in. wide, interior with removable tray. $1,665 £740

William IV rosewood games table with reversible chess/backgammon board. $1,845 £820

Mid 19th century French work box in satinwood and kingwood, satin lined, 34in. high. $4,500 £2,000

Regency games, writing and and work table in calamander wood, about 1800. $4,500 £2,000

19th century Biedermeier ebonised and parcel gilt globe work table, 96cm. high. $4,500 £2,000

Early 19th century rosewood games table on turned and reeded legs. $13,500 £6,000

Victorian pine and cast iron school desk and chair. $65 £30

Victorian mahogany writing table on turned legs. $200 £90

Late Victorian bamboo writing desk. $340 £150

Early 19th century oak slant top school desk on brass cup castors. $550 £245

Maplewood centre or writing table, circa 1850, 42in. wide. $565 £250

Small inlaid mahogany writing desk, circa 1900. $565 £250

Rosewood writing table, circa 1900, 32 x 24in. $630 £280

Flemish or German walnut writing desk with crossbanded top, 1880-90, 40in. wide. $630 £280

Late 19th century Swiss walnut writing desk, superstructure with four small drawers. $745 £330

Late Victorian mahogany writing desk. $775 £345

Victorian oak library table with leather top, American, 19th century, 38in. wide. $785 £350

An Oriental black stained and hardwood writing desk, circa 1900. $900 £400

English rosewood bonheur du jour inlaid with foliage, circa 1900, 47in. high. $1,010 £450

Regency rosewood library table with plate-glass top, 112cm. wide. $1,055 £470

Late 19th century ebonised and burr-walnut bonheur du jour, 41in. wide. $1,070 £475

William IV rosewood writing table, 1ft.5in. wide, circa 1835. $1,170 £520

'Regence' contra partie boulle writing table, circa 1850, 32½in. wide. $1,780 £790

Regency mahogany secretaire writing table, 43in. wide. $1,800 £800

Mahogany and satinwood crossbanded writing desk, circa 1890's, 37in. wide. $1,855 £825

Mid 19th century red boulle bonheur du jour, 81cm. high.$2,140 £950

Edwardian mahogany Carlton House writing desk, inlaid with satinwood stringing, 103cm. wide. $2,200 £980

Mid 19th century French parquetry display cabinet on writing stand, 153cm. wide. $2,250 £1,000

George IV mahogany writing table, circa 1820, 3ft.3in. wide. $2,475 £1,100

19th century serpentine front crossbanded bonheur du jour, 3ft.3in. wide. $2,755 £1,225

Art Nouveau mahogany writing table with drawer. $2,925 £1,300

George III mahogany tambour top writing desk with side carrying handles, 45in. wide. $3,060 £1,360

Mid Victorian walnut and marquetry writing table, 55in. wide. $3,150 £1,400

Antique mahogany architect's table with ratchet writing surface.
$3,600 £1,600

George III satinwood bonheur du jour on square tapering legs, 2ft.3in. wide.
$4,500 £2,000

William IV mahogany library table with green leather top, circa 1830, 5ft.4in. wide.
$5,400 £2,400

'Louis XV' kingwood bureau plat of serpentine outline and leather top, circa 1900, 59in. wide.
$5,515 £2,450

Bonheur du jour in kingwood and Vernis Martin, circa 1900, 45in. wide.
$9,000 £4,000

Regency rosewood and cut brass inlay library table, 151cm. wide.
$9,225 £4,100

Late 19th century ormolu mounted kingwood bureau plat, 53in. wide.
$11,700 £5,200

Art Deco galuchat and ivory, lady's writing table, circa 1930.
$27,000 £12,000

French Regency writing table and filing cabinet, circa 1720, 5ft.11½in. wide. $63,000 £28,000

William IV mahogany teapoy with octagonal hinged top, 14in. wide. $440 £195

Victorian rosewood teapoy on tripod base.
$450 £200

A Victorian mahogany teapoy on a carved base.
$450 £200

Early 19th century rosewood teapoy on platform base with vase feet.
$505 £225

Georgian period teapoy in mahogany, 20in. wide, circa 1825. $790 £350

George III satinwood teapoy on splay feet with brass cup castors.
$1,125 £500

Regency mahogany teapoy with ebony inlay, 29½in. high, circa 1810.
$1,690 £750

A delicate, early 19th century, rosewood teapoy complete with caddies.
$1,690 £750

Regency simulated rosewood teapoy, lid inlaid with cut brass scrolling, 15in. wide.$2,025 £900

Edwardian oak and metal banded trunk. $55 £25

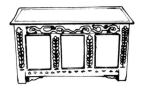

19th century oak hall chest with carved panels to the front, 188cm. wide.
$225 £100

19th century camphorwood trunk with brass straps and corners. $335 £150

George III mahogany silver chest with brass fittings. $620 £275

A Portuguese Colonial teak coffer, circa 1800, 4ft.6in. long, 2ft.1in. deep, 2ft. 3in. high. $675 £300

Camphorwood chest, heavily carved in the round, 44in. wide. $720 £320

19th century Dutch burr-elm veneered chest, on bracket feet, 48¾in. $900 £400

Early 19th century Chinese red lacquer leather coffer with brass lock plates, 31in. wide. $2,815 £1,250

119

An Art Nouveau marquetry oak wardrobe, 137cm. wide. $630 £280

Early 1920's walnut and ivory wardrobe, designed by Leon Jallot, 193cm. high. $745 £330

Early 19th century French cherrywood armoire with brass fittings. $1,900 £845

Rare painted wardrobe, by Wm. Burges, 1870's, 53in. wide. $2,100 £935

19th century breakfront mahogany wardrobe with satinwood banding, 111in. wide. $2,250 £1,000

Ormolu mounted scarlet boulle armoire with arched cornice, 46½in. wide. $2,585 £1,150

19th century Dutch armoire in oak, rosewood and ebony, 6ft. high. $5,175 £2,300

Solid walnut breakfront wardrobe by Peter Waals. $5,195 £2,310

Rosewood armoire by Louis Majorelle, 103in. high. $11,250 £5,000

Victorian marble topped washstand on shaped legs. $100 £45

Victorian stripped pine washstand with a tiled splashback. $135 £60

Victorian marble top washstand on a walnut stretcher base. $170 £75

Victorian mahogany wash cistern complete with bowl. $270 £120

Early 19th century inlaid mahogany basin stand with hinged cover. $360 £160

19th century rosewood pedestal basin stand. $420 £185

Early 19th century mahogany corner washstand with undershelf. $450 £200

Early 19th century mahogany combined washstand, pot cupboard and commode. $725 £320

George III mahogany campaign washstand/writing desk, 28in. wide. $1,465 £650

WHATNOTS

Victorian inlaid walnut three-tier corner whatnot with turned supports. $280 £125

19th century ebonised etagere with brass embellishments. $315 £140

Rosewood whatnot, circa 1850, 28in. high. $540 £240

William IV rosewood whatnot with a three-quarter gallery, circa 1835. $810 £360

Victorian walnut whatnot of serpentine form. $810 £360

A mahogany oval etagere, with three tiers, circa 1910. $845 £375

Victorian walnut rectangular three-tier whatnot, 107cm. wide. $990 £440

Victorian papier mache whatnot. $1,575 £700

Parquetry three-tier whatnot with lobed upper shelf, stamped Holland & Sons and W. Bassett, 21½in. wide. $2,250 £1,000

Large solid rosewood Anglo-Indian wine cooler, circa 1840, 30in. wide.
$450 £200

Mid 19th century 'George III' oak wine cooler on stand, 26in. wide.
$475 £210

Early 19th century mahogany wine cooler of sarcophagus shape with paw feet. $675 £300

Regency mahogany open wine cooler, 28in. wide.
$745 £330

19th century Dutch marquetry wine cooler on cabriole legs with brass carrying handles. $900 £400

Regency mahogany octagonal wine cooler.
$1,015 £450

Early 19th century sarcophagus-shaped mahogany wine cooler with original lead lining. $1,035 £460

Georgian mahogany wine cooler, 18in. wide, circa 1820. $1,180 £525

Regency mahogany wine cooler with oval fluted lid, 27½in. wide.
$8,100 £3,600

INDEX

124